A Practical Guide to Collecting Civil War

BURD STREET PRESS
SHIPPENSBURG, PENNSYLVANIA

This Burd Street Press publication
was printed by
Beidel Printing House, Inc.
63 West Burd Street
Shippensburg, PA 17257-0152 USA

The acid-free paper used in this book meets the guidelines for permanence and durability of the Committee on Production Guidelines for Book Longevity of the Council on Library Resources.

For a complete list of available publications
please write
Burd Street Press
Division of White Mane Publishing Company, Inc.
P.O. Box 152
Shippensburg, PA 17257-0152 USA

Library of Congress Cataloging-in-Publication Data

Mesker, James P., 1949-
    A practical guide to collecting Civil War / James P. Mesker.
        p. cm.
    Includes bibliographical references.
    ISBN 1-57249-143-4 (acid-free paper)
    1. United States--History--Civil War, 1861-1865--Collectibles--Handbooks, manuals, etc. 2. United States--History--Civil War, 1861-1865--Collectibles--Catalogs. I. Title.

    E646.5 M47 2001
✓ 973.7'075--dc21

                                                                2001035560

PRINTED IN THE UNITED STATES OF AMERICA

Contents

This section is an overview, with actual examples of how to collect Civil War antiques on a budget, where to go, what to do, whom to see, and how much money to bring.

What is a Civil War antique? How do you define your focus when your money is limited? How to read existing publications and know your time periods.

This chapter covers where to find Civil War antiques by giving examples. Different kinds of things you should be concentrating on are noted. Stamp shows, flea markets, coin shows are all covered in these pages.

This chapter covers the all-important question of what to do when you find a Civil War antique. It provides strategies that may help you determine whether you should buy the antique and how to tell if it's worth the price.

Well, now that you've gotten your great buy home, what do you do? How do you enhance its value with no additional cost and have fun with this hobby at the same time?

Learn how to collect edged weapons and get to know the United States ordnance patterns employed at the time of the Civil War. Be aware of other nations who imported weapons to both the North and South. A word about price and market values for the beginner.

Illustrations

Preface

While researching the topics for *A Practical Guide to Collecting Civil War* I found that authors like Richard Taylor Hill, Francis Lord, and William A. Albaugh III all used contemporary primary sources. These authors illustrated examples of items that were available, both commercially and from the government. For example, an item illustrated for sale in *Harper's* is reproduced as an example in Francis Lord's *Civil War Collector's Encyclopedia*; William Albaugh uses city directories and period newspaper articles to identify his offerings.

The Time Life Civil War publications and the photographs used in the "Jack" Davis publications carry Civil War artifact collecting to an exciting, oh! enticing spirit of "gotta get one." Many dealers will point out that their item offered "for sale" is the same as the one pictured in, for example, *Echoes of Glory*, on a specific page. This does not mean you have the particular object depicted in *Echoes of Glory*, or even the same thing.

If you read the bibliographies of Civil War collecting publications, you will find the items, pictured or illustrated, are sometimes from the same collection, or collector. That may be a reason to say "All Civil War fifes look like the one in Time Life *Encyclopedia of Collectibles*." It is more accurate to say: "The fife pictured in the several publications is the same fife," only.

The intent of this book is to expand this field of collecting to items not previously recognized as Civil War or related, and not necessarily high-priced (and/or valued) pedigreed items.

Introduction

This narrative is for collectors who want a return for every dollar they spend; have an interest in the Civil War, or early American military; and budget a certain amount of money every week to spend on their hobby—that is, disposable income, not investment income. Directed at the persons who feel the urge to go to every antique flea market, gallery, and show within a one-hundred-mile radius of their home, this book is unlike any other catalog, book, narrative, or description of Civil War antiques published so far.

This book will make collecting Civil War antiques basic and affordable for you. Just pay attention to the strategies described and to the situations encountered and then apply them to your own collection, after some preliminary research. In addition, you will see Civil War-era and related items that are representative examples of the pedigreed types you see in other books. These will be used to illustrate the various categories of collecting that are covered in this book. They will also help you to understand how to verify such examples by using books identified as necessary references.

In addition to these books, some tools you will need, for the moment, are a coin identifier book, a stamp book, a library card, and a magnifying glass "to see the fine print." The Civil War period could be 1860–61 through 1865–66, not just Sumter to Appomattox. A familiarity with household items, 19th-century ways, utensils used, how tasks were accomplished, fashion, and inventions is also important. Now where to go with these tools? That will be just about any place that hints of Civil War: flea markets, antique shows, coin and stamp shows, and reenactments. Each of these offers its own advantages.

As you develop your own experiences you might hear that finding an uneducated dealer is a real advantage. However, that is not always the case. Many times such a person will inflate the price of an item that has even a hint of Civil War. In a flea market or antique mall, in particular, this inflation can be as much as two hundred percent or more. Some dealers may find a Civil War or Civil War-related item, having no idea what it is, and price it according to the local market. Instant gratification being your objective, if you can maintain a budget of $20 for these items you absolutely have to have, go ahead and gamble that they are probably the $80 ones you saw identified in a book a month ago. You can come out ahead value-wise. Another "Civil War on a budget" success!

Chapter One

Civil War Antiques Defined

For the purposes of this book a Civil War antique will be broadly defined as any instrument, or civilian or military artifact made during the Civil War era (1860–1866) or just before. Through 1866 because the hostilities continued after Appomattox. Many books and price guides provide list upon list of the articles you may find, including those used in civilian life. The main categories of possible purchases are covered in detail in later chapters.

Confusion may be the watchword when picking out Civil War artifacts. Your actions may be colored by references to pristine, top-quality, excellent condition items—those seeming to be the only criteria for making an investment in a Civil War collection, according to popular authorities. Limited funds, however, does mean not following this advice. It is a lot easier to lose $15 on a mistake than $500. Remember, you are not a serious collector, at least not yet. A relic dealer I know still talks about the rare $500 button his inexperienced collector wife bought that languished in his $5 relic box for years.

Define your focus by deciding what appeals to you and do some budget-buying in that category. If you don't like it, drop it. Refine your tastes as you go along. For example, under the heading of paper, stamped envelopes (in stamp collector parlance called "covers,") from Johnson's Island, a prisoner of war camp, can be had for approximately $150, depending on condition or signature. You, however, might only be interested in a representative example of such an article, and there are some mutilated Johnson's Island covers, usually fronts of the envelopes only, or with dates possibly just post-Appomattox, for example, which you can pick up for about $35. Great historical value!

You can buy mutilated covers and similar items as historical examples of those pristine, mint condition pieces every day of the week,

Examples of mutilated covers

Counterclockwise from the right: Johnson's Island cover (front only) $35, 1996. If excellent condition and in complete form, according to Scott's *Specialized Catalogue* criteria,[1] priced approximately $350-$800 for a similar item. Confederate prison cover, $2 in 1997. Flag of Truce cover (South to North), $25 in 1996. If excellent condition with the requisite period stamps, both Confederate and Union, can be valued at about $1,200 each. Camp Douglas cover (Union prison), North to South, $35 in 1998. If excellent condition worth upwards of $800.

Identification tags

Parmelee identification tag, "tool check" style purchased for $5 in 1996. If it were the "coin" style shown in popular catalogs it would be listed at $950. As it is, this little publicized type is worth around $225 because it has been researched to identify the soldier. Webb is both an ID tag and a corps badge combined and was valued at $95 in 1997. Battlefield relic; from the flanks of Pickett's Charge. In this condition, can be valued at around $1,000. If the soldier was a fatality its value increases.[2] Compare these tags to those found in *Lord's Civil War Collector's Encyclopedia.*

and never have the urge to "move up." After all, you are out to have some fun, not to make a profit.

At stamp shows, remember you are not a stamp collector. You might buy items in the dealer's miscellaneous pile as examples or just desire to have a particular item in your collection. When you combine that cheap period cover with a wallet of the period, suddenly the two individual items of under $20 each now equate a mini-collection of personal artifacts and are worth a bit more than individually.

Identification (ID) tags are another desirable personal artifact you may want to collect. The most desirable are Confederate, but this would be a very rare find. Union tags can be purchased for practically nothing. People call them tool checks because they look like something that existed into the 20th century, a great misnomer for these desirable pieces.

A disc of German silver, in an oval configuration, with any type of patriotic motif, usually with a name and a town or city, state or other form of geographical identification (eliminating those with phone numbers and sometimes addresses), may just possibly be a soldier's or veteran's ID tag.[3] It will probably take a little research, but that is why you have a library card. With a little working knowledge of your public library and/or interlibrary loans you can take something that you picked up for approximately a dollar (the highest I have ever paid is $5), and increase your awareness of its value.

Make yourself aware of the geography and try to locate a roster of the soldiers in an area. If you are lucky, you'll find out that the guy on your tag was a soldier. Premium catalogs supply identification of regiment and company and then sell those items for hundreds of dollars. You can do the same type of research and end up with an item worth about $250 retail with a $5 investment.

Try to avoid getting too caught up in the concern for top quality, pristine condition items. You're not going to have much fun in the hunt. The premium items are available for sale in quantity. All you have to do is pick up an auction catalog or go to prominent Civil War shows and buy the best at the highest dollar with all the guarantees involved. If you're like me, you only have $20. See how much you can get, how far you can stretch that budget, and how much history you can buy.

One weekend we went to a flea market and an antique show in a park where everyone said no Civil War items were available. I found nine items at one dollar each. Granted, the items are not too significant, but the fact is nine dollars bought nine Civil War or Civil War-related pieces: three photographs, three GAR (Grand Army of the Republic) postcards, a minie ball, a rubber button, and a brass button fragment. Somehow they'll be put to use.

To get lucky in the hunt read, read, and read the pictures in the picture books. Go to your library, gather the magazines and the books with pictures. Read the words, put the pictures in your head. It will come in handy, for example, when you're looking through a pile of CDVs (cartes de visite) at $1 each and you think you recognize a face.

CDVs, an inexpensive method of portraiture, originally intended for use as visiting cards, started in France in 1854. This became a fad that soon swept across the Atlantic to the United States. Many CDVs were issued in the thousands like today's baseball cards. CDVs were unlabeled because at the time of issue people recognized the person on sight. That isn't the case today; consequently the cartes de visite are usually a low-priced item at a place like a flea market. A dealer will have a pile of CDVs priced inexpensively—your choice—and he'll label the items "very old, from the 1800s." If you're familiar with the faces of well-known people from that period, eventually you're bound to find an image of one of them. Believe me, the first time you do, it will be exciting![4]

Make yourself aware of the revenue stamps on the backs of some CDVs. Dealers may say "there's an old stamp on it," and you end up paying for the presence of the stamp in addition to the price of the piece, but it may be worth it. Some CDVs that were purchased at a flea market for one or two dollars may sell for $300 to $500. I obtained several at low prices; they are not worth hundreds, but definitely ok.

Collecting Civil War for resale? It's the investment, top quality question again. But whether you want to have some fun and trade with a group of guys you know, or whether you want to sit on part of your collection and, later, sell your items in order to buy something you then will want, keep reading.

You can go to premium antique shops in your town and make an investment in the items the dealer can't quite guarantee. These objects tend to be discounted because the dealer is cautious of his reputation, and you can pick up something you might have a lot of fun with or need to fill a spot in your collection instead of that multi-hundred dollar, documented antique with a pedigree as long as your arm, which you can't afford anyway. A good deal all around.

Something else that's always a good deal is Confederate money. Do not buy the parchment paper you see being sold. You can get those sheets at your park service stores for about one dollar on a thousand. These inexpensive, mutilated examples of real Confederate bills, or perhaps counterfeits contemporary to the period, are always good to have on hand. The same goes for bonds. Bond coupons are usually very low priced, so pick them up.

Collecting Confederate postage stamps? It is difficult to tell the real Confederate issue from that issued by other sources. Only a serious collector of Confederate postal history can tell the difference. Those Confederate postage stamps and cancellations have been duplicated from the war to the present day. If they're cheap, buy them, keep them. People do love them, and want them. A few years ago people didn't even know they existed.

A collectible with a Southern origin, Southern imprint (non-military included), is another thing. Pre-Civil War and post-Civil War published items with Southern sentiment are available and very nondescript. When you find such a thing for less than $20, buy it and keep it. For example, I picked up some "Maryland, My Maryland" sheet music at Gettysburg in July 1995, which had been published in a Southern state, below the Mason-Dixon Line, in 1861. This item is becoming more and more difficult to find.

Keep in mind that you want to have a clear picture of items that existed during the Civil War. Try looking at newspapers from the period on microfilm in the library. You need to know what existed, what might be available, and what soldiers and the civilian population were using at that time. Read the personals, want ads, and illustrated materials. More than likely, you will see something you never before identified with the period of the Civil War. One or two price guides have

CDVs (cartes de visite) of ordinary people

Good condition. $1, $2, $3 in 1996-1997. Each lists for around $4 in excellent condition. Union enlisted man. Replaced mounting, good condition, unidentified and unarmed. $1 in 1996. List for excellent or outstanding is around $35. Portrait of general in uniform. Identified as Wade Hampton, Confederate. A photographic, slightly faded image (as opposed to a photographic rendition of an engraving, or a printed CDV). Good original condition. Lists for $250 in excellent crisp condition.

"Maryland, My Maryland" sheet music

This sheet music with lyrics written by James Ryder Randall, a "Baltimorean in Louisianna," shows the Maryland state coat of arms and expresses sympathy to states' sovereignty. This music was published by Miller & Beacham in Baltimore in 1861 just prior to Fort Sumter's fall and before martial law caused by the Baltimore riots. The words to this version were a summons to arms in defense of states' rights. The military government moved to suppress this anthem. That resulted in the publication of Union parodies such as "Maryland, My Maryland," published by Lee and Walker of Philadelphia and "Maryland, My Maryland," published by Charles Magnus and Company of New York (a version which shows an illustration of an old man whispering in the ear of a young Southern Belle).

been published recently with lists of these items. Familiarize yourself with the pictures; if an item is listed and you don't know what it looks like, do some research.

This approach also helps with post-war veteran's artifacts. Examples are those associated with GAR (Grand Army of the Republic), the Boys in Blue, the Loyal Legion, and the Republican Club. These men lived on through the 1880s, at the very least. ID tags from this period can still be valuable. Don't shy away from them just because the date is a post-war year, or the piece indicates the individual's profession. For collecting ID tags keep your purchase in the $1 to $5 range.

The examples of artifacts written about in chapter one are certainly not the only Civil War items you can purchase on your budget. However, they may be the most commonly encountered. There are others that cost a few more dollars: edged weapons, firearms, equipment, and accouterments. We will discuss these in later chapters and tell you how you can manage to collect them on a budget.

Chapter Two

Where to Find Civil War Antiques

Civil War collectibles may be found at Civil War reenactments or living histories. These events are usually well advertised in many communities, especially those with some kind of Civil War history.

Usually a sutler's tent (or three or four) can be found at these events, where all sorts of things are for sale. Granted, there's a lot of duplication and reproduction. You're buying in a market, after all.

You'll get an idea of the myriad of representative artifacts that are available. Since some are real and some aren't in this particular marketplace, you will learn to distinguish between the good and bad. For the purpose of your collection, however, consider this: if the items are $1–$2 buy them and have some fun playing with your new toys!

The facsimiles that abound in the sutler's tents are there for reenactors to buy and use in their battles and living histories. They tend to be of good quality and perfectly acceptable to fill a space in your collection. This might be where you want to consider buying a more expensive item, like that Confederate shell jacket you've always wanted—only this time it's a reproduction for around $75 rather than several thousands of dollars for an original.

Reenactors are always searching for period artifacts, some of which can be bought elsewhere for less money. Flea markets are a good place to find bottles and inkwells—paraphernalia that reenactors like to use. They love to use the real thing when they can get it. Sutlers are selling reproductions—period types. If you want to buy a Civil War bottle or porcelain ale bottle attributed to, for example, the Petersburg area, you would spend approximately $100–$125 at Civil War shows in a Southern town.

After going to the area flea market in Cleveland three times a week for several years, I have been able to find that very bottle (or a representative example thereof), for around $3-$5. Inkwells too, not from a battlefield, but exactly the same type. So, when you go to a Civil War show, you can fantasize that your Cleveland bottle could really be Gettysburg, Appomattox, or whatever you want it to be. In fact, the guy standing next to you has probably done that very thing and probably can't tell the difference.

Flea markets are really excellent places to buy Civil War on a budget. Do some reading first, however. Make yourself aware of the types of buttons that were in use for both civilian and military clothing. Also, what types of clothing styles were used, like vests for working in the fields. Know the hats. Each geographical location had its own fashion. You can distinguish a Southern from a Northern individual by looking at his clothing. Lighter weights, colors, double-breasted, fancier styles all determine the locale.

I had the experience of not being able to buy Civil War on a budget at Gettysburg over the July 4th weekend. This is one of the largest Civil War shows and reenactments in the nation. Everything was much too expensive for me at the show tables.

But, in Gettysburg, just like in towns all across the United States, you can find little antique galleries, also known as antique malls, with little spaces where a number of people have a variety of antiques for sale. Now, you might think that in Gettysburg the people have to know what Civil War is; however, the truth is they have such a glut of Civil War, some don't care, as long as an item is sold at a reasonable profit.

I found one such mall during my visit, and purchased a 36-star GAR lapel pin for $1 ($12 at the Civil War show tables up the street) and some sheet music printed in a Southern state at $3.50 each, one with martial marches, and the other was "Maryland, My Maryland." The total price was $8 with a 10 percent discount. Then I went to the Gettysburg Visitors' Center and saw a copy of that exact piece of sheet music on display in the Park Service museum. An item like that could run $50 today,[1] especially in the Civil War shows going on near the little mall where I bought this sheet music.

A Civil War antique show is not usually the very best place to buy period items. Go to learn, see examples, compare prices. For actual buying, try a stamp or coin show instead, where prices for Civil War-related items will usually not include a premium just for being Civil War. For example, a Confederate pass does not belong in a stamp show, and so it only costs $20.

I can go to the Garfield-Perry Stamp Show here in Cleveland in March and pay catalog ranges for "across the lines" (either North to South or South to North) covers and Confederate postage and other such philatelic items, or I can spend time going through a miscellaneous pile and see Confederate and Union paper that is governmental issue, like pay warrants, requisitions, and passes. These are relatively

Civil War-period bottles

All purchased in Cleveland. Average cost $3, 1996–1997. If a battlefield relic, price may be approximately $45 each.

discounted because they have no philatelic (as pertaining to stamp collecting) value. Some dealers separate the contents of their stamped envelope covers to sell separately in a miscellaneous category.

At a coin show, besides period coins, you can find mutilated coins; for example, coins with some punch holes, which may signify their possible use in the Copperhead movement (especially if they are United States large cents).[2] Old flying eagle pennies with some punch holes could indicate a Southern makeshift button.[3] Pennies were cheaper than buttons, which often had to come through the blockade in the South. These can be verified by the date, and one side being worn and the other side mint or near it.

Chapter Three

Civil War Collecting Strategies

A typical weekend in a Civil War artifact collector's life is a busy one. Here's one from last winter as an example: There are two shows today, a dollar admission flea market and a once-a-year paper show, at a senior center. No glitz, no publication, just little shows in close proximity to each other.

We hit the road as soon as possible to be there when the doors open at 9 a.m. (at the flea market). We go directly to the book seller (already knowing he will be there). We pick up for $5 *The War Between The States* by Alexander H. Stephens, published in 1867. Consider a book, or anything, about the war published in that year, contemporary.

And there just happens to be, priced at $10, one of the books everybody looks for (it's not that common): *The Great Rebellion*, Volume 2, by J.T. Headley, published in 1866. The engravings alone are worth more money than that. They were marked "Entered into Congress" in 1865 and they are fabulous.

In the course of many visits to many shows and markets you will see these engravings ripped out of the book and matted for $10–$30. It's terrible to say that the parts are worth more than the whole, considering the historical aspects of the book, but sometimes that's the way it is in today's antiques market. The book is a decorator's dream. Plus, it is a vital source of reference because it cites military reports. When you're done, depending on the condition of the volume, you could remove the pictures and frame them. Though Alexander Stephens' book has only three or so pictures, it too is worth buying. The book was written by a leader of the Confederate government. Even in poor condition, it's a historical example.

Okay, that's 30 minutes (you have to hurry) at the flea market, and there's another show down the street. When the doors open, take a quick look around. We finally scope out two cabinet cards, patriotic photos of

Book advertisement

Period ad for Stephens' book delineating importance for that era.

Period books

1866 Headley and 1867 Stephens books, $10 and $5 at a flea market.

soldiers for $20–$25, which is a bit high, but one's a good image and can't be passed up unless there's something better.

If you have a budget, don't buy just to spend your money. But, if you have a budget, and the price is good, and you love the piece, don't hesitate. Stay friendly with everyone. You might get a tip. Just like on this trip, a trading partner whispered that a certain table has a roster book of Pennsylvania troops that's a little out of his price range today.

At first we thought it was a Bates' index of officers of Pennsylvania troops, which is worth quite a lot of money on its own, but it was priced at $40. It turned out to be The Adjutant General's Report, 1864, for Pennsylvania troops in the field, all regiments, all localities, and includes expenditures, etc. and only has a couple of missing pages. Worth considerably more in Pennsylvania.

It's research material. Not reedited, not accidentally omitting anything. A primary source. There's an ID tag in my collection (purchased for $5 at a flea market), that, in my library research, appeared only two times. But in this book, because the story is more complete, it was found

Roster book of Pennsylvania troops

$40. Slightly soiled, with some pages torn. List price in good to excellent condition is $185. Can also be considered for purely historical value, condition notwithstanding.

Henry B. M'Kean..........	June 22, 1861...	10 Li...
George S. Coleman........	July 11, 1862...	....
R. H. M'Coy...............	June	Resig...
A. A. Scudder........,.....	Mar	.....
Charles Bower......,......	June	Su
Z. Ring Jones.............	June	u
A. J. Atkinson........ ,.....	July 31,	h...
J. L. Bishop...............	Aug. 15, 1862...	10 Su
	Mar. 14, 1862	

Identification tag

C.W. Bower ID tag with roster book open to his name.

Carte de visite

Printed CDV of Judah Benjamin, secretary
of war of the Confederacy, $12.50.

that the individual named on the tag was actually in three regiments through the end of the Civil War. Reedited or reproduction research material may not give you benefits like this.

If the person you're buying from has one thing, he may have another. Sure enough, there was a full page page of Magnus CDVs. Magnus published printed CDVs (as opposed to photographic), patriotic envelopes, song sheets, maps, and more in the Civil War period. I bought the cheapest one because my budget was running out.

How do you decide what to buy? It all depends on what you like. A friend came across a picture from the 1940s that he thought was of a Civil War veteran because of the medal he was wearing in the photo. On the back the image was identified with the name, the date of birth, and the date the photo was taken. He had a feeling the medal was a Gettysburg reunion medal, and we had no way to verify that at the time.

After buying it for $3, we took it home and found that it was a 75th reunion medal. If you were buying for resale in Pennsylvania that would be a quick $30. That's really Civil War on a budget! (Note: This is Civil War related, not period, but that's his focus, what he likes.)

Chapter Four

Enhance Your Collectibles' Value

After you purchase an item, you can enhance its value by finding out more about it!

Start in the genealogy section of the local library. They have names, addresses, ancestries, and everything that goes with looking up your family history. Military rosters, especially for the Civil War, may be documented for the particular locale. Additional documented information on individuals that enlisted and units that were formed in the general area may be available. Artifacts tend to stay in or return to the area of their origin.[1] Soldiers, if they lived, usually went home to their families after the war. You should be able to find artifacts where you live that are easily identified and documented with just the information in your local libraries or with your purchased references.[2]

These artifacts may include coins of the Civil War period that have counter stamps, that is names or initials and geographical locations. Also, published materials like song books, testaments, and tracts may have names on them. Verify the name, making sure you have the spelling correct. Clarify it, remembering that Spencerian script makes it hard for the eye to identify letters, and a lot of this writing is Spencerian. That's the first step in your puzzle solving.

Once you get a name from your Civil War-era artifact, go to the library prepared to spend a little time. If you happen to find a Smith, you are going to be there for a week. Check the index to the rosters of soldiers, then go to the book or microfilm of the roster indicated. Find where that regiment or unit was mustered. You will usually find it came from a fort or training camp in a certain area. The information about the companies will also say where they were mustered—a city, a county, or a town.

We purchased a song book, *The School for the Fife*, instructions for playing the fife, an 1856 publication by Elias Howe, Jr.[3] This book had a name on it and an address of William Thorpe, Bath, Ohio. Checking the genealogy section of the nearest library, we pulled out the Ohio Rosters, and found several William Thorpes. That meant looking for those men who came from areas surrounding Bath, which eliminated six men. A William Thorpe, 19 years old, who was a musician, a fife player in the regimental band, was in the very last book.

The unit was raised in Norwalk, Ohio, and mustering efforts were at Camp Cleveland. Camp Cleveland was not that far from Bath. Some people might say, "How do you know that's the same William Thorpe who was the fife player in that unit?" Do you really want it not to be? You have eliminated all the illogical conclusions! By the way, the song book, at the flea market, cost $5.

Photocopy the information you have that's pertinent to the item you are researching. Put it all together, and your little $5 investment has given you a personal artifact with documentation (the photocopies). As far as "how do you know?" remember, we're not big dealers and our stuff isn't going to Christies. You can be fairly certain that the conclusions you have drawn are the correct ones.

Never discard the excess information you may have copied, because, if you find *one* item in an area where you are flea marketing, there may be others. We found a whole group of the ID tags mentioned in chapter one in the immediate geographical vicinity of a flea market we frequented last year, and used some of the research two or three times.

Buy budget references, especially if they will help you in your research area. This came in handy at a rummage sale. People were grabbing what looked like GAR uniforms, coats, and vests, but we were only fortunate enough to get a hat, sold to me as a cowboy hat. It was a Stetson, yellow cord decorated with acorns, no badge, just holes where a badge would have been on the front. We finally settled on an $8 price for this mint condition GAR Civil War veteran's hat. It even has the head strap that comes around the back to keep it from blowing off. I found an ad in the old 1902 Sears catalog reproduction purchased several years ago, selling the very same hats to GAR members.

Guys usually put their names in sweat bands, and there was a name in this sweat band. An officer's index of Civil War people is available in the genealogy library. This index is for the whole Union army's officers, even 100-day men, from a second lieutenant rank and higher.

Fortunately, only two matching names were found. Checking the geographical area closest to where the hat was found, I identified our man and verified his name by checking GAR membership rolls and camp numbers. It was a GAR hat, in mint shape, identified to an individual. You can't stop there, however, because if you frequent flea markets and antique shops for any length of time you can pick up a GAR cap badge

GAR hat

The seller thought it was a band hat.

for anywhere from $16 to $35. I found one for the hat and now have a wonderful item for $24 identical to those already pedigreed items sold at an exclusive Civil War show for $150.

Another item found at a local antique shop was a 46-star flag. It looked pretty good. The price was right, sewed-on stars, little damage. Gigantic garrison size, it could be military oriented. I noticed a name along the flag pole side binding. This happens quite commonly. Usually it is very faint due to laundering. Next to the name was a GAR (Grand Army of the Republic) star. Paid $35 for it, quickly found the individual in the Ohio roster, and have turned down $500 for my flag, but I bought it on a budget and can afford to spend some time enjoying this beautiful piece of history.

A footlocker

Purchased for $25 in 1997 at a Cleveland city flea market from a woman with Maryland license plates. The carving appears to be legitimate. What is it? You decide.

Chapter Five

Collecting Edged Weapons

Edged weapons is a category of high-priced goods, highest return, greatest investment for budget buying. Let's start by looking into something no one ever shared with me, and it took me ten years of research to find out: "What's a Civil War sword and what isn't?"

The answer lies in research and reading of the most basic kind. Find a reference book with some terminology, some history, and some pictures. *The American Sword 1775–1945* by Harold L. Peterson, published by Ray Riling Arms Books, is a good example at $45.

The author begins with terminology, covering fullers, grooves in the blade; the ricasso, the small square area near the hilt; the tang, the part which is inside the hilt. He gives a description of hilts, the part above the blade; and covers the grip, the part your hand touches; pommel, the very top; guard, that goes to protect the hand. The funny curved end of the scabbard (the sword cover) is called the drag because it protects the sword from dragging on the ground.

Peterson gives a brief history of the subject before giving detailed descriptions of swords as they were made in each year, including pictures. His cataloging of swords is so complete that people name the sword type they own by the Peterson number that describes it. I bought a Peterson #38 before buying the Peterson book. They call them P38s.

Doing your homework with references like this is a good thing. You need to be able to readily identify Civil War or post-Civil War use or manufacture of any suspected Civil War sword, including the inspector's marks, acceptance, US and manufacturer date. If these features are missing to any degree, value will be affected.

The United States government, the Regular Army, from about 1840, only had a few patterns or types of swords and there were only a few government-sanctioned manufacturers. The swords the government issued were primarily NCO, cavalry (Dragoon), artillery, and musician

23

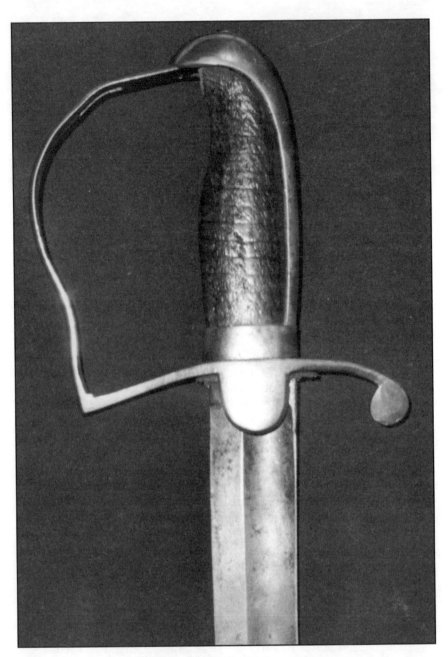

Example of a Peterson #38

$90 in 1996. Single, unstopped fuller on curved blade with wood handle and brass guard, in average to good condition. If excellent, lists around $300. In this condition approximately $180. It would be priced considerably higher in presentation grade with etched blade.

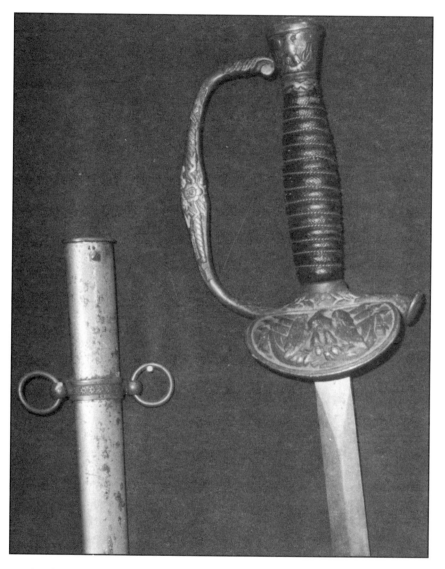

Officer's sword, 1860 pattern field, and staff officer's sword

Paid $90 in December 1996 at a neighborhood junk store. Poor condition, no marks other than US and the year somewhat visible on the blade. A good space filler in better than relic grade. If relic, it would actually go for $125–$150.

swords. There are also some United States (issued 1840, 1850, and 1860) field and staff officers' swords that are very expensive and are rarely encountered.[1]

All swords issued by the government have little inspector's marks, the US stamp of ownership, and the date they were produced or at least received into the army. This type of labeling basically starts with some uniformity around 1840. It dates and guarantees United States use of an edged weapon. Other edged weapons, however, were produced earlier than 1840, either in the United States or somewhere else entirely. When you are looking at Civil War swords, you will find an incredible amount of these in the officers' sword category.

Officers, by United States Army regulation, were to provide their own swords.[2] This is a large area and stretches over a long period of time. Many of your gallant old officers in the North and South brought to war the sword their great-grandfather used in the War of 1812, the Mexican War, or even the Revolutionary War.

The West Point graduates had swords that they fancied and had either bought for themselves or received as gifts for graduation. Purveyors provided officers with a wide selection of swords, most of which were manufactured abroad. They were fine European swords, predominantly French, German, and English, and so marked; therefore, you're not going to be able to track down the date and usage with the inspector's mark, and you're not going to know positively that it's made in the United States. It will only be a type.[3]

Many of these types of officers' swords are extremely high priced and they often involve an 1850 European pattern, which could be obtained throughout the 1880s. Know your patterns and the dates to which they belong, along with the countries that produced them. Most of these swords you encounter will be high in price. Horstmanns, for one example, are still going for $550 on the low end. For the beginning collector, this means maybe three to four months or more of your Civil War budget. Stay away from them! Learning about these weapons takes some time, and a lot more knowledge than can be contained in this volume.

There are some affordable weapons out there. You need to know your patterns and your styles. At some flea markets, swords in the price range of $50–$125, which may have some Civil War usage, can be found. These are the non-officers' blades issued prior to the Civil War in the United States, or in a foreign country, as just described. They are collectible, somewhat cheaper, and you can guess that they could have been used during the Civil War since they were made before the war occurred. Why pass on them if they're offered within the right price range?

Beware of turned metal, of stainless steel blades that look a little pitted, or crude, and cheap-looking guards. There's a lot of costume

Sword reproductions

$8–$25 in 1996–1997. Indian, Spanish, and Pakistani-made.

material out there that might fool you. Look at the handle wrap; is it the right material or do you only see the wooden pineapple?

Many reproductions were not made as fakes but facsimiles. This is the difference between, for example, Confederate swords, brass hilted, selling for $300 versus $3,000 for the authentic piece. Not for you. The reproduction may be $35–$400; the genuine sword will never be available again for $100–$125. But, as stated, there are other categories of swords that are good legitimate deals until the more desirable sword comes along or your budget expands.

When planning a big purchase, deal only with an established expert/dealer of military objects. They will more often than not give you a guarantee or a return policy. Ask politely ahead of time if they don't volunteer that information. Hold this type of expenditure for a special occasion.

On the positive side, for collecting edged weapons on a budget, there are always bayonets. With a few exceptions, like confirmed Confederate and the Harpers Ferry Saber bayonet, you can afford a Civil War bayonet. You can find saber bayonets for under $100, and what people often call spike bayonets, or socket bayonets, for around $35. This may go a long way to satisfy a Civil War collector on a limited budget.

Obtain an early Bannerman catalog. Bannerman was an early army-navy surplus provider and issued catalogs for years and years. You will find these catalogs (in rough shape or reprint form because you don't want to spend a fortune) invaluable in correctly identifying a variety of Civil War bayonets—and, of course, non-Civil War bayonets.

Bannerman catalogs are well illustrated. Pay close attention to the details, and you will find these books are a great learning and research tool to use in your edged weapons collection.

One type of bayonet, the saber bayonet, was often carried by Zouave units in imitation of the French.[4] A common type is called Yataghan[5] for the curve of the blade. Remember, a Yataghan blade style bayonet has the lower hand guard curling toward the grip, or straight, if you are looking for a Civil War-period piece.[6]

Those with the curl toward the point are post-Civil War, after 1866. Saber bayonets may have proper markings as described earlier in this chapter, or no markings at all, as many French ones in the market. You can pick one up for approximately $85 dollars, a Zouave type, saber bayonet with nice French markings, usually a model 42 pattern which will be stamped "IMP."[7] If you can get that for under $100, that's not a bad deal.

Spike bayonets can be found for $35–$50. These are the bayonets that look like a wrought iron spike, faceted or not.[8] A good suggestion is to purchase the .69 caliber socket bore rather than short bayonets (which may have been clipped) with a .58 caliber socket bore. By the end of the Civil War, .69 caliber was all but obsolete.[9]

Always look for a US marking at the base of the blade forward of where it curls up to fit on the barrel of the gun. That's about all there is in US markings to identify your purchase. There are earlier bayonets in about the same price range that were used in 1812 or even the American Revolution.[10] They may have British proof marks and tend to be about the same length, plus a little wider and more triangular. They qualify for possible Civil War usage depending on the firearm, and are usually budget priced.

Caution: Look out for Edwardian spike or socket bayonets being sold as Civil War. Remember any British military piece will have the monarch's symbol over the crown, and you're not going to find a Civil War-period item with Edward as the king. This is a very good example of why you have to know history. Victoria is the monarch you want to see on your British bayonets.

Bannerman catalogs

$20 in 1996.

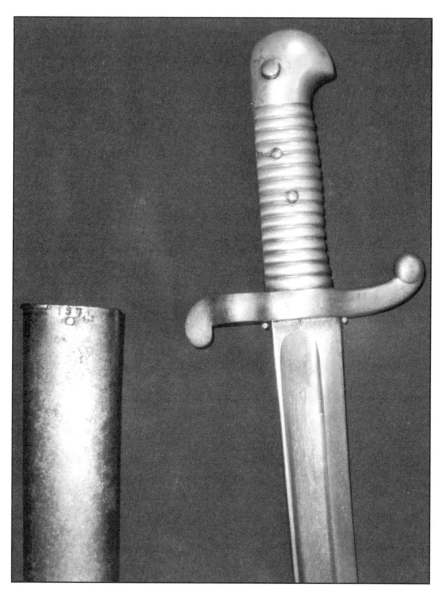

Yataghan-style bayonet, model 1842[11]

$85 in 1996. Excellent condition. French Imperial markings; a good buy. Adopted by both sides in large numbers. French and Belgian bayonets have often been encountered with marks ground off and represented as Confederate.

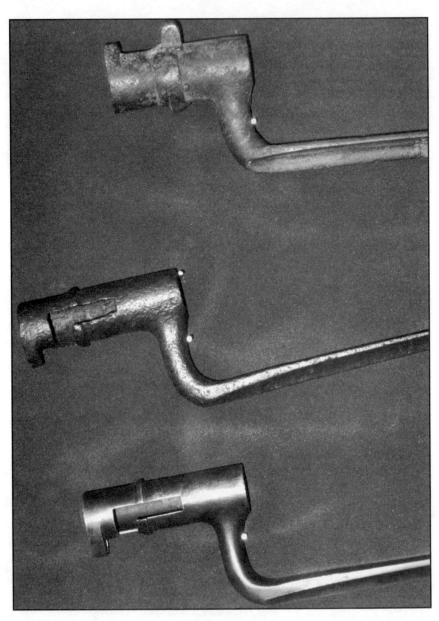

Bayonets

Post-Civil War bayonet for Trapdoor rifle; the cost was $35 at a flea market in fall of 1996; fully marked, included for identification purposes only. Relic condition British Enfield bayonet, Civil War period, battlefield find, valued at $100. Socket spike bayonet with retaining clip for United States pattern 1842 rifle and musket, US marked; purchased for $65 in 1996.

Chapter Six

Collecting Firearms

Most collectors desire a musket when they start accumulating Civil War items. The best advice is to proceed with caution because artifacts in this category usually cost a lot.

You can tell yourself a lot of lies along the way, but somewhere down the line you may find out you've made a mistake. Then you will be on your way to learning the differences in the firearm items presented for sale in the Civil War marketplace.

Purchase a copy of *Civil War Guns* by William B. Edwards, published by Stackpole Company. This book sells for about $35 at an antiquarian book fair. Edwards is very clear in his descriptions, and his book includes illustrative photographs. The book *The Great Guns* by Harold L. Peterson and Robert Elman, published by Grosset and Dunlap, is useful for background materials and explanations (out of print, find one at a book sale for under $5). Several catalogs or guides list information about inspector's marks, serial numbers, and production years. Use *Flayderman's Guide To Antique American Firearms and Their Values* for comparative values (published by DBI Books, Inc., $29.95).

The Edwards book is painstakingly researched and looks at Civil War history through the sights of the guns being used at the time. It exhaustively covers the subject, and includes quantities of guns obtained and delivered, foreign purchases, both Confederate and Union; it has detailed descriptions of markings plus illustrations. This is information you need to have available. In fact, the knowledge you gain from just looking at the pictures and the captions in this volume will be invaluable.

The difference is in the details, as you can see by the following example. Someone says, "Got this real beautiful Confederate musket here, British Tower. You know that Towers were Confederate." You (guess who) stand there and the price is right. It's exactly how much you have in your pocket, right then. Oh boy, big purchase. You buy it.

You think, "Hey, I've got my Confederate musket! Why, it says 1862 Tower. Oh wow, it's wonderful and look at that, the barrel markings even say SC—South Carolina."

Later, you show it to somebody and he says, "Oh, that's a real good Union musket there." How does he know? Well, on the breach is the inspector's mark for the port of New York, on the Union side. SC are his initials and they have nothing to do with the state of South Carolina.[1] Guns with SC stamped in the stock, in the wood, were imported into South Carolina from abroad and are displayed in many museums.

If you paid more than $800 for your new musket, grin and bear it because Tower with that description can still be purchased at around half the price. If you managed to do that consider it a good deal. Plus, if the gun has the inspector's marks as described, you've probably got a real American Civil War Enfield.

You will find from your reading that Enfield is a major type (pattern) of foreign, contract musket purchased by the Union and the Confederacy during the Civil War. Both London manufactures and Birmingham manufactures were imported and can indicate Civil War use.

Tower is the British government's acceptance mark for guns assembled at the Tower in London. However, according to Edwards, post-1860 Tower marked guns don't singularly indicate British military acceptance. Tower was stamped on the trade muskets as well; placed there to indicate first quality. Memorize the marks as outlined in books like *Civil War Guns* by Edwards.

Be aware that dealers may go to England and purchase a number of Enfields and present them as having been used in the American Civil War (Northern and/or Southern) when they actually had no use in the conflict at all. This is especially true when you find symbols like little arrows with a VR under a crown, dated after 1861, which indicates British military use during the time of Victoria. Watch for British Enfields made at Enfield and so marked on the lock; they are probably not of American Civil War vintage either.[2]

Experience, combined with research and patience, will help you when you are planning a large purchase like a musket. This means patience when looking to find exactly the right item. The advice that applies to swords also applies to firearms: save up, then go to a reputable dealer. Don't worry, however, even if you get stung or make a mistake because there will be a market for the piece eventually. Firearms are very popular, especially for trading. Again, cheap equals buy, when considering legal pre-1898 weapons.

Let's examine this in a little more detail. For example, a lot of East India material is being sold as Civil War, especially muskets, Brown Bess type. A Brown Bess, being associated with the American

Revolution, was made through the mid-19th century.[3] The muskets are decorated with lion's heads or little foxes. They are export pieces for East India Company, Hudson Bay pieces, not to be confused with American Revolutionary artifacts. They are good, really beautiful, but have nothing to do with the Revolution.

These weapons are excellent pieces in themselves, unless you paid $1,000 or more for one as a Revolutionary War-era musket. You probably have an India Mutiny or even post-India Mutiny gun, about 1858. These guns have nothing to do with the Civil War and nothing to do with the Revolution.

There are some pieces in this category, however, that could be Civil War related. Currently in our possession is a P1839 Brown Bess that was purchased with the implied connotation of the American Revolutionary War—basically sight unseen, unresearched, no information on date of manufacture. (Don't do this, it's very risky.) We knew, however, it was cut down, as was the custom post-war, especially in the South. It came from a collector friend and the price was right at $125. We researched it with British publications, not US. You can find them in your library.

With these budget references we were able to verify the marks on the gun as indicating probable Confederate use of this Brown Bess. Guns of that model with those marks numbered about 30,000 in quantity. Some were used by units in the British military including the Royal Marines during the Opium Wars. Thousands were purchased by the Southern Confederacy.[4]

What is the gun? Well, after a thorough cleaning a date of 1861 showed on the breach. I believe we have a real Confederate Brown Bess even though it was cheap because it's cut down. Although not a 100 percent positive identification, this representative piece looks good over the hearth.

Information like this is difficult to find. You must understand the inspector's marks, alpha and numeric, and information about Tower and the arrow marks on weapons. And here's more detail: the last model of the Brown Bess to see American Civil War use appeared in 1839.[5]

Using the knowledge acquired from your reference books will help you collect firearms and other artifacts. Remember your date and remember to concentrate on buying American rather than British, French, or Belgian. Only buy the British, French, or Belgian weapons if you are reasonably certain of Civil War usage as a result of your research—after all, your overall focus is the American Civil War.

You'll probably follow the desire for a musket soon with the urge to own a pistol. A very costly prospect, in some cases. Take a look at Flayderman's *Guide to Antique American Firearms and Their Values* to see what your budget can handle and search your library for a book

Brown Bess Musket

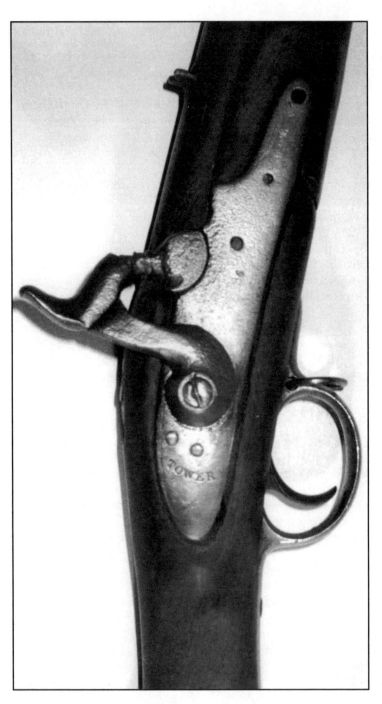

Pattern 1839⁶ Brown Bess, purchased with the implied connotation of the American Revolution, in fact, turned out to be probable American Civil War use by the Southern side. $125 in 1995. Poor condition, but intact. Value in decent condition $400-$500.

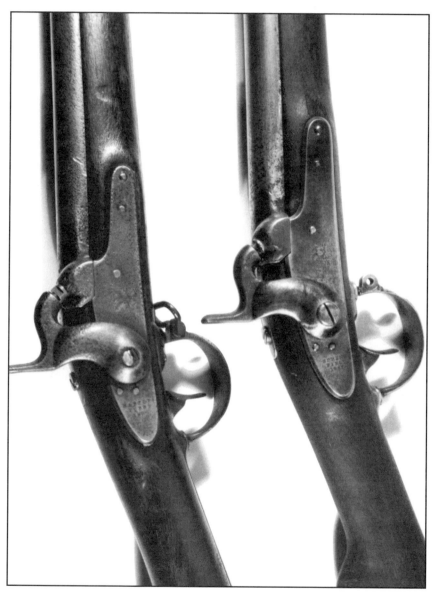

Budget firearms

Purchased for under $200 since 1992.

with background and some technical aspects. Flayderman may fit that bill too, depending on the type of handgun you're after, especially when you begin this part of your budget collection.

Not long ago, most people claimed that a Smith and Wesson Army #2s had no Civil War usage. The historical specifications, however, said yes. Suddenly, after selling mine at a substantial profit, I discovered that now, everybody knows what they are because of all the recent popular literature showing that very pistol. Apparently these guns are being shown because they are really common and are identified specifically to the period.

There are some affordable pistols in the market place for Civil War on a budget. Take a look at the Prescotts, the Smith and Wesson #2s, 1½s, 1s, colt pockets, Whitneys, Belgian pin fires and boot pistols. Pay close attention to the serial number, however, because all of these types saw extensive use both before and after the Civil War.

If you like Colt pockets, look up the range of serial numbers for the years you're interested in and find a suitable gun within that range. Before is arguably okay, but not after. If the gun was made before the war and it exists today, it existed during the war. Colt, for one, provides a book of serial numbers and dates for a nominal sum.[7] We purchased one for $8 at the Colt Museum in Gettysburg in 1996.

If you're into the aesthetic aspects of the American Civil War, you should buy relic grade or relic type, battlefield dug, so you can be sure you have an actual Civil War piece as opposed to the mint condition example of a Civil War piece. This is fortunate for the on-a-budget collector because, with a few exceptions as already noted, relic grade pieces are somewhat less expensive.

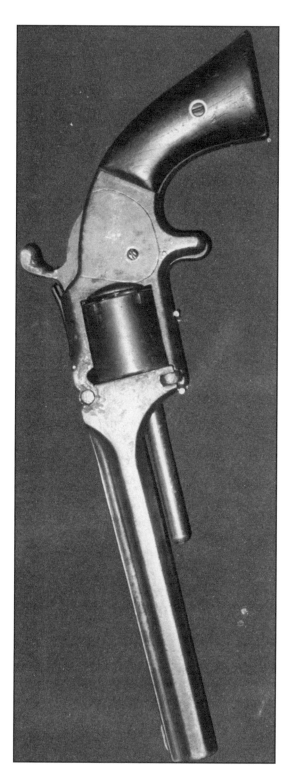

Smith and Wesson Army #2

Repurchased for $165 in July 1996. Serial #14063 with welded hammer. Note: This was my very first. Originally purchased for $25 in 1986; sold for $75 in 1992, and had to have it back when the opportunity presented itself.

Budget handguns

All purchased for under $275 since 1992.

Chapter Seven

Collecting the Civil War Soldier's Personal Items

Personals are another area of focus that a budget collector should not overlook. Personals include everything a soldier might have carried, even for recreational use. It's an aspect of collecting Civil War that is much more domestic than government military issue like guns and swords.

Consult one of the popular Civil War price guides to see what's on their lists for personals. Comb the sutlers' tents during reenactment weekends. Try Francis Lord's *Civil War Collector's Encyclopedia*, published in 4 volumes, volumes 1 and 2 in one book for $19.98, the same for volumes 3 and 4.

Items that are customarily available in the Civil War marketplace have been listed in popular Civil War literature and can be easily recognized. Look for books with photographs of artifacts. The pictures are usually very effective, and your ability to identify personals suitable for your collection will be greatly enhanced.

Most personals can be had for a reasonable price, even cheap if you're astute. This collecting area includes anything the soldier brought or shipped from home to camp to make himself more comfortable. Personal artifacts, such as twists of tobacco, religious items, sewing kits, razors, writing kits, chess sets, games, flasks, cards, dice, and candles fall in this category. Personal items used every day in civilian life would naturally find their way into camp even if some, like playing cards and dice, had to be concealed because both armies officially prohibited gambling for enlisted men.

Let's take chess sets as a good example of this type of artifact. Lord's *Civil War Collector's Encyclopedia* states that chess playing was rare in the army. However, some books illustrate pages of chess sets belonging to officers and POWs. Many Brady/Gardner photographs show officers playing chess. One of our sets comes from a Union officer in Libby prison and is so documented! We have another period set with

Chess set

Purchased for $75 in 1996. Identified to prisoner at Libby Prison. Similar one identified to a man from Indiana was purchased for $50 in 1998.

a British maker's name that could have been a British export to the South; a traveling set with a canvas board that folds into the box. Checkers are said to have been much more popular, but we have yet to come across a Civil War checkers set, or even dominoes, which like checkers were thought to be a popular recreation in camp.

In camp, the soldier needed things to write with and write on; he needed stamps; he needed pen and ink. He was frugal. We have seen envelopes on which across the vacant half of a ripped stamp is written "ripped stamp." This usually means that a soldier could get away with sending two letters for one three-cent stamp and stretch his supplies. In the interest of being frugal, the soldier also needed some way to carry all his things to keep them dry. So, he had to buy other items that weren't issued to him, like wallets, housewives (sewing kits), and more.

If an item was light, small, and compact he couldn't live without it; a soldier carried it somehow, somewhere. And if a soldier could carry it, like a collapsible drinking cup, it is now a Civil War antique. The contents of a soldier's haversack[1] typically included a tintype or two of his family, food like hardtack, a housewife, Bible, tin mug, razor, eating utensils, money, and more. If you walk down Caroline Street in Fredericksburg any day after noon and visit the antique shops, you might just find that a spoon from the 1860s, for example, worth 50 cents at yesterday's flea market is suddenly worth around $10 at one of the shops. We saw some not long ago for $4.

The collapsible sets existed in the Civil War period and are still made today, but some of the others really have Civil War usage. You find out by checking the Federal Contractors books or the lists in Lord's *Encyclopedia*. Look up the makers' names. We found several spoons that appear to be government contract because of the maker's name. Now you are moving up from a spoon for a dime to a spoon at $5 that was possibly carried by a soldier.

Other personals include razors, but not everybody carried one. Not all American men shaved, especially not rural Americans. Razors never became United States government issue until the 1870s. Look for razors with patriotic decoration. Some were carried by regular soldiers for personal use or more enterprising individuals who made money as the camp barber. Razors could be purchased from the sutler, and in the case of some of the more affluent individuals, were deposited with the barber for their personal use.

In fact, reports state that some people had a new razor for every day of the week and a shaving mug too! Depending on his status, how much money he had, how important he wanted to be, or was, his sword, his razor, and everything else would be purchased to befit the soldier's station in life.

Housewife from the Tim Daley Collection

Period utensils from the Tim Daley Collection
Reenactors love these types for their authenticity.

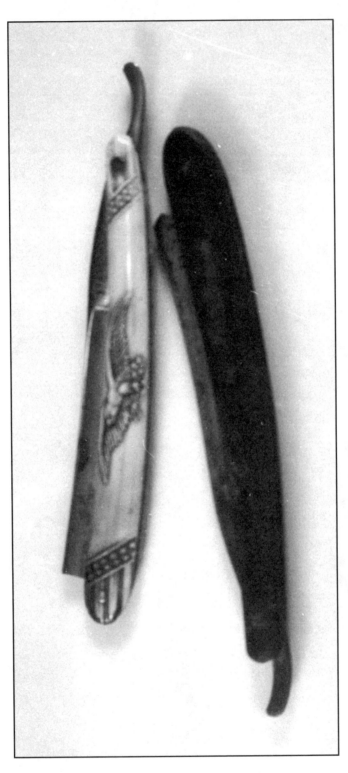

Patriotic razors, North and South

The Union razor is pictured in Lord's.² A big plus for value. They both cost under $35. The "Death to Yankees" razor cost $25 and was bought from a collector friend. It is a period razor and properly marked. Value without "Death to Yankees" about $40.

Remember that soldiers were drawn from both rural and urban settings and there was a great discrepancy between the accouterments of the rural and urban soldier. Urban men tended to fit better into regimental life than country boys. Sometimes they were better educated, and knew what they needed, like a shave once a week, a haircut once in awhile, shoes blackened, or a bath. They wanted a little recreation, like singing, smoking, card playing; and they needed medicinal items to protect against the diseases which were rampant.

Remember, they were a marching army in various climates and could carry only so much for so long. Based on collections of soldiers' correspondence several episodes report a soldier discarding his knapsack with all his personal belongings and then writing home for replacements over and over again. Use a little imagination and look for the logical. What would you need if you were there? Then research and identify the pieces that you can buy on a Civil War budget!

For the collector of budget personals, the patriotic razors shown in the photograph are desirable because they are available and reasonably priced in the razor market, but obscure in the Civil War shows. Lord's *Encyclopedia* pictures the eagle razor two times and, as there is a mystique attached to "as pictured in Lord's," it is generally sought after at a premium price. Shop the flea markets for items like this.

Wallets are another desirable personal item. There is no real set style or pattern. Some show patriotic motifs and others have military unit embossments. Some are just plain, utilitarian. There seems to be no decisive size, or color. They may be lined or unlined. Wallets identified as military tend to be premium. Patriotic motifs hold the middle ground. Plain period wallets can be purchased for as little as $5, depending on condition.

The five wallets in my collection right now are all representative of the Civil War period and include patriotic, military, and domestic styles. A favorite is the plain, utilitarian wallet bought from someone who had purchased it from a defunct museum collection. It is identified to a soldier critically wounded, and contains newspaper clippings regarding the soldier's demise. $17.50. It's great!

A close second is the 9th New York Heavy Artillery wallet. The men of the 9th New York were the heroes of the battle of Monocacy, where they fought as infantry. This is a very prized piece, in very good condition. A $9 buy. It's a rarely seen item, so we can only guess at what the retail price would be. But, as always, it was purchased on a budget.

Budget personals

Match tin, razors, pipes, coins, wallets, and script. Maximum purchase price $20, from 1992 through 1998 at area flea markets.

Chapter Eight

Collecting the Civil War Soldier's Equipment Items

When you consider the well-equipped soldier and what you can buy that was his, start with the common militaria: uniforms, insignias, and all the associated accouterments. These are popular, though expensive, military items. In this classification are hats, or kepis, pants, boots, booties, underwear, and vests. Budget collecting really isn't going to allow you to buy a shell coat. Pants, however, are up in the air. You can decide how attractive a pair of rotting old pants are, and exactly how much you want to spend on somebody's old underwear and socks. They just don't look good hanging on your wall.

You can still pick up a few things on a budget. For some of them, you are not necessarily looking at traceable Civil War military usage, but you are going to be looking at definite Civil War style and pattern, especially for uniforms and accouterments. Some items were army surplus into the 1870s and beyond, but are good representations. You can still purchase one that's perfectly acceptable, even desirable, at the level at which you want to presently collect.

"Be wide awake." A chapter could be spent on just this phrase. Check on all the details and prove every one of them. Look at the buttons, the labeling, and more. Look up the Federal Contractors. Look at the uniform photos from the Smithsonian archives. These should have a great degree of accuracy. Read any Bannerman catalog. Try to find a button book like *The Collector's Encyclopedia of Buttons* by Sally Luscomb, published by Crown Publishers in 1967. This reference, for obvious reasons, is very important when looking at uniforms.

An example of this importance is the dating of the M.C. Lilley Company. Many say that M.C. Lilley is only a late post-Civil War name, 1872 and beyond. But, did you know that M.C. Lilley was providing buttons in the 1860s,[1] according to *The Complete Button Book* by Albert and Kent, one of my budget reference books? Rule of thumb: Do the

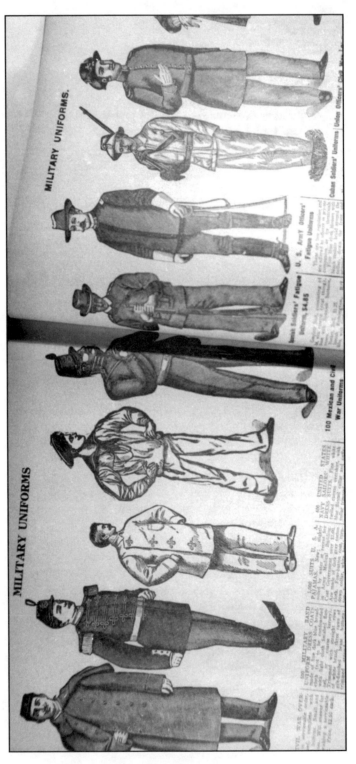

Bannerman Catalog page

January 1938 shows Civil War surplus: coats, hats, uniforms. Great for identification of period type.

Kepi hat

research yourself, because the memories of others may be wrong or incomplete.

Some of the more common artifacts available for budget purchasing are hats. These cloth items are sometimes falling apart, and you're definitely not going to wear them to do your yard work. The items will be too fragile, and more than likely too small, due to the smaller stature of most Civil War citizens. Zouave hats are unheard of and you don't run into slouch hats that often. The hat you'll see most often is called a kepi.

Kepis are very distinctive; they are the style hat you see in all the movies, the books, the prints. An ideal place to find a kepi is a large flea market or a large antique show. One of my first kepis was purchased at a large show in a shopping mall.

When you are looking for something like this, price will be the governing factor. Remember, kepis were made for schools, bands, private military institutions, and the army as a fatigue cap, a daily uniform

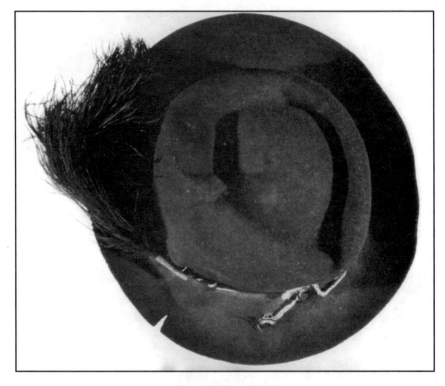

Slouch hat

cap, into the 1890s. They can even be found advertised in *Youth's Com-panion*, a popular young person's magazine, circa 1898. It's really, re-ally hard to differentiate between, for instance, an Indian War piece of the late 1860s to mid-1870s and one attributable to the Civil War. There are some tailoring differences: crown height varies, curve and width of the brim changes slightly, and lining and labeling are naturally different.

Books are available to help you understand these differences. But, these are things we're not too concerned with at this level of collecting. If you find a Civil War-looking hat, no matter what condition, brim size, crown size or whatever, and it runs around $65 to $150, that's a pretty good buy for a representative piece.

You may come across a kepi in a large Civil War show that a dealer says is from the Indian War or perhaps Spanish-American War. Civil War being the premium and the others being run of the mill, don't be intimidated by this. A good Civil War kepi will cost upwards of $2,800. Price depends on condition, ornamentation, and identification. When you get into identification for these items you are talking about escalating the price even more. When it comes to hats, stick to buying something that may have been a good old boy's school cap, but yet is the style or pattern you are looking to find.

You can find some of these hats on a budget. Cultivate your sources. A collector friend said he had a kepi for me, a Civil War style, but the brim looked a little bit like Spanish-American War. We met and the price turned out to be $150, which was tendered immediately before he changed his mind. It was the good old Union blue, with the crushed, tarred cardboard visor, the chin strap with buckle, and crossed rifle buttons from the New Jersey National Guard.

Crossed rifles mean the kepi is post Civil War, and since the buttons are National Guard, it can be narrowed down to later than mid to late '60s because National Guards were more like the militia raised by counties. In 1872 crossed rifles became the mark of the infantry and replaced the hunter's horn.[2] It became totally universal in the American army by 1875. A 1872 kepi doesn't mean that it isn't Civil War pattern, just not period use. Not Civil War exactly, but what a deal!

Actual period use goods are still out there. Sometimes you can find campaign hats or slouch hats, usually felt-covered cardboard. They tend to be more expensive because of their rarity. Hat ornaments tend to be inexpensive and common, but don't spend more than a few dollars each for them. Between the reenactors pieces and post-war pieces which are

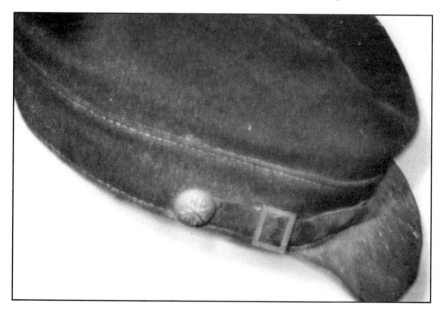

New Jersey National Guard kepi
$150 in fall 1996.

New Hampshire second lieutenant's coat

antiques in themselves, it's hard to accurately pinpoint the time period. In other words, identifying the artifacts—unless you have a maker's mark, the proper references, and familiarity with variations in patina— is very difficult and often confusing, so buy low or buy relics.

Another frequently mislabeled item is a militia coat (beware of band uniforms). Civil War militia coats do exist, and are available. Price is definitely a factor, and also, you want to find something that is attractive. It's a "you want it; you've got to have it" situation; and if you are not really particular about pedigree (it's a representative piece, after all) and the price is right, go ahead. And the right price means, do you have the money available or are you going to postpone the mortgage payment?

We came across a militia coat, roughly 1865–66. It's a transitional style, combining a 5-button sack coat type with the 1859 regulation collar, with nice second lieutenant bullion bars on the shoulders. The coat has no name or identifying marks except "New Hampshire" on the buttons and the name of a Civil War period button manufacturer.[3] We traded about $250 worth of material for it, since it was a late Civil War uniform coat. Since it's not United States government issue, there is no readily available design comparison, let alone price point, but it's a great budget buy nevertheless.

A little harder to evaluate are boots and booties. The prices run from $65 to $150. You'll find evidences of boots, both Confederate and Union. Look for mislabeled items because not everyone knows

Relic buckle

Union marked US. $45 in 1996.

what they have on their tables or in their shops. We were at an upscale show and found a woman who had a pair of boots labeled "little boy's boots." On examination, they had pull-up straps, hobnailed wooden soles, wooden heels, leather tops, and an eagle with a shield along with seven stars in two scrolls on the top fronts. They sold for $50 and look great! Another collectible boot is the style of shoe commonly worn by the soldier.

Belt buckles are also a very popular category of military accouterment. In fact, belt buckle collecting is a hobby all its own, especially with regard to Civil War. We bought them as bonafide relic pieces off a battlefield. They're affordable at $45–$85.

If you want to buy these buckles new or almost mint at a high dollar you should consult experts who can point out the differences in the die cracks from one buckle to another, and can identify their origin by a centimeter's difference in the positioning of a letter. Before purchasing a buckle, find a reputable source, save up and buy that buckle with a guarantee, or look for a guy with relics and buy a relic buckle on a budget.

The same advice applies to buttons, another category suitable for Civil War on a budget. As mentioned in chapter one, a dealer friend of mine has a button in his $5 box that his wife purchased (obviously without a guarantee) for $500, believing the dealer knew what he had. These are not unusual situations in this area of collectibles.

Be aware of some of the intricate details of buttons and pay attention

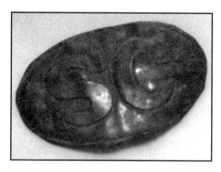

Confederate belt buckle

From the collection of Joseph Ostervich, who is recognized locally (Cleveland) as an expert in the field. Retailed out at about $750 in 1998. We know he paid less when he bought it.

to the marks on the backs, also called backmarks. Use a ready reference guide that helps you to date the period or time frame of the button you found. The Wyckoff *United States Military Buttons of The Land Services 1787–1902,* published by the McClean County Historical Society in Bloomington, Illinois, is an invaluable guide. This reference book details the minute differences in the military buttons available, such as the age difference between the serifs, the scripts, and the blocks, the initialing on the eagle breast shield of the common military buttons which may span 65 years of military history.

Research a list of button manufacturers and their way of marking button backs. A Connecticut button manufacturer put "Superior Quality" on his buttons during the Civil War and then again on the same design in the 1960s. This is a confusing area and you need to study references like *The Complete Button Book* by Lillian Albert and Kathryn Kent, published by Doubleday in 1949. Look for it at an antiquarian book store or sale.

Buttons are still easily accessible artifacts for collecting Civil War on a budget, both in relic and non-relic condition.

Recently I bought, for $8, a small grab bag of military style buttons at a tag sale. The bag contained military style dress buttons with the exception of one Civil War hard rubber, metal shank naval button with horizontal anchor[4] which price guides list for $40–$75.

Chapter Nine

Collecting Paper Items of the Era

Book shows, nostalgia shows, and especially stamp shows are really good sources of Civil War paper items: letters from home to soldiers, government form paper, newspapers, photos, and similar pieces. Stamp shows are fabulous because the dealers are, for the most part, only concerned with philatelic value, the value of the stamp itself (fortunate for the Civil War collector on a budget).

A good reference is the *Scott Specialized Catalogue of United States Stamps* from the Scott Publishing Company. This imposing book is extremely useful in determining dates of interesting covers, especially when it comes to Confederate stamps. It's expensive, so look for one that is a few years old for type and date referencing only. For instance, do you know which stamps were issued and commonly used in the 1860s or exactly what Sanitary Fair stamps look like? Or that the Confederate postmaster general was John H. Reagan? And what about counterfeits? The *Scott Specialized Catalogue* will give you some of the information and background you need when you go shopping for Civil War at a stamp show.

When purchasing covers from an individual at a stamp show, inquire as to whether or not he still has possession of the contents. It's been my experience that usually the seller doesn't care about the letters. They place more or less a nostalgic value on them, paying little attention to the historic value of the contents.

Sometimes you can buy a batch of letters separate from the covers for a nominal investment. This might mean that you will spend a good deal of time trying to match them to the envelopes, if any of them do match. Since a lot of Civil War history was played out in letters, you might find a pattern in the letters and covers of a dealer you frequent, and discover they are all part of one particular family. We have found that many stamp dealers aren't aware of these circumstances because

Sanitary Fair stamps

they are usually just interested in the stamps, or the cancels, and they did not look at the names. You might want to construct a family tree around such correspondence and get a picture of the relationships between the letter writer and his family.

After purchasing letters and covers separately over a three-year period, we started looking at all of them and discovered that they were mentioning the same names. It was a whole family, the sisters, the brothers, and the last names of their respective spouses. We found that three of them were killed in the war. Matching the right letter with the right cover or envelope was a little bit tricky, especially when the soldiers seemed to have written their letters on the same day, in the same units. Perhaps during a rest or on a rainy day in camp a man would write five or six letters in one day to five or six different last names, all related. That was a find!

The price of the eleven letters with covers was around $35, a great buy for priceless history considering the story it tells about a family with three soldiers killed in the war. Be sure the condition is good, the people can be identified, and the writing is completely legible. What good would it do anyone to have such items and not be able to read them?

Other collectible items include published material, such as little pamphlets, periodicals, and books, and sheet music. Anything printed from the 1850s through the Civil War period or 1866 can qualify.

You can find these items on sale at flea markets, bookstores, or junk sales. Sometimes there's a name or maybe a name and address. A price below $10 equals a good buy! If you can, find where the booklet was printed. You can go to your local library to look at the rosters of the state's troops to try to find out whether the guy was a soldier.

Usually, if a man stayed home all the time he didn't need to identify his belongings. But, if he was buying things like dime novels or periodicals for entertainment or instruction and he put his name on them, chances are he was a transient person, aka a soldier. When you find the item, look up the name, identify the man as a soldier[1] and turn your $5 to $10 into a $50 value, as we did with the Civil War song book, previously mentioned.

Government form papers are another avenue to pursue, and period examples are very popular. If this interests you, start by collecting representative examples in any condition, ripped, water stained, or foxed. By the time you are ready to move up to a better quality of paper items, you will have decided for certain if you want to continue collecting these items. Check the US government and Confederate form numbers against those illustrated in *Lord's Encyclopedia* to be sure that you are buying period authentic pieces.[2]

A small selection of 1860s stamps

The *Wildman* letter and cover collection

You can't collect everything. You have to go with what you like. I like the military aspect, but tend, in this area of collecting, to focus on anything considered to be Confederate memorabilia. This includes Southern imprinted documents, publications, tax forms, tax payment receipts, gas bills for the Richmond Gas Company in the 1860s, and more. Finding items like these on a budget is a thrill you can't pass up.

At a very large flea market we found some CDVs (photographs about the size of a business card) of unidentified Union enlisted men, and a couple of identified senior officers. The seller cut me a price of $35 each. The revenue stamps on the back were in good condition, but they basically had no photographer imprint, and the cancel on the stamps either couldn't be read or it wasn't tied to the piece itself. They were the only items with a good price, a little high, but we decided to look down the line and come back and buy.

My wife who was looking with me, came across a display selling costume jewelry from the 30s, 40s, 50s, 60s—really nothing in the Civil War field. Lying on the table, there was a CDV album all by itself. The binding was period. I got very excited, opened up the first page to a soldier and closed the book quickly.

Now comes the moment of truth, how much is it? The price tag said $29. After politely asking, "What can you do for me on the price of this today?" The reply was $25. We didn't dare look at the rest of the book. There was one soldier for $25, plus an entire album which is worth something even empty. Another vendor had a similar CDV for $35.

When we opened up the album, we discovered seven soldiers, and a politician. All the soldiers are identified to a family. It's a quality piece, photographers, revenue stamps, and everything. Further, my research found the family and the soldier, all from the geographical area of the photographers. Two of the men died of disease while in the army during the war. What a $25 investment!

Song book by Howe identified to William Thorpe, Regimental Band, 55th Ohio

64

Government form paper

Telegraph, Discharge, Commission—purchased for under $35 each through 1998. The condition is fine, and the price is within budget.

A few examples of paper items ideal for a Civil War collection

Most purchased for under $10 through 1998. One was found between the pages of a testament purchased for $1 at a used book store.

CDV album, as described in the preceding paragraphs

CDV is short for the French *Cartes de Visite*, visiting cards that were a popular 19th-century collectible. They are almost as popular today.

Chapter Ten

Concluding Tidbits on Collecting Civil War Memorabilia

This chapter offers some general hints on the process of Civil War memorabilia collecting. Not only what to look for, but how to behave, and what to anticipate in the market place.

You should be courteous, polite, and act like you know what you're doing by respecting the merchandise. Proper behavior means: don't butt in on people, don't interject yourself into another person's deal, and never denigrate someone's merchandise. You know the kind of person who does this: if it's theirs it's great and good; if it's yours it's common and trash.

Some people are trying to earn a living or augment their income, and they are not necessarily collectors. In some cases they are collectors looking for some things they want and getting rid of things they are tired of, so there is room to bargain. Basically, though, many of them are there for a quick turnover, and that works to your advantage when it comes to negotiation.

When you are shopping for collectibles, keep your eyes open and your ears in tune. Listen to conversations about what people have found and where. Don't be too obvious, because you're not the only person looking for these items. Look at everything, don't assume that a certain person isn't going to have your type of artifact. You could be surprised, for a dealer with predominantly different type of material could have just the piece to complement an area in your collection.

You should cultivate sources by dealing with certain people. If they're in this for a living and you are a collector, they will start looking for items you like and save them until you show up. (If they like you.) Don't make this a source of anxiety; if you don't show up, you don't. This is supposed to be your recreation, your reward. It's not another job.

If there's a trunk filled with junk, dig deep. Many, many a nice item has been found hiding under a pile of trash, inside a jewelry box, between the pages of a book, behind a picture frame.

Hunt, hunt, and keep hunting. Your collection will not be completed in three weeks. Some people have been doing this type of accumulating of Civil War memoribilia for 50 years and they are just now getting their collection the way they want it. Again, it's supposed to be entertainment, a hobby, something to enjoy. It isn't going to happen instantly.

Remember that this is a sense game. All of your senses have to be in tune; you've got to feel that piece; you've got to handle it. You have to have your eyes wide open, scanning everything. Don't see something that isn't there, especially if you're talking about spending $100 or more. Don't try to read something that doesn't exist into a piece. And don't say it looks good and this is as close as you're going to get to the real one, and then buy it. It will only turn out to be a great and expensive disappointment, particularly when you show it to someone else and obviously it isn't the piece you hoped it would be. Just stay focused and keep plugging away.

We used this approach recently when finding a Civil War drum at a local market for $115. I got excited and insisted to my wife that we had to have it. She, however, didn't like it. (I mean, how could she do that?) Didn't like it. Didn't give me any money. Two months later, we found another drum for $185. We bought it. The differences between the two drums: the first one was an approximate example, late period, maybe; the other one was the real deal, with provenance, and a history provided from a long cultivated source, and (compared to retail value) a budget purchase too.

Don't get unrealistic expectations. You won't always find the item you are looking to buy. Don't try to do too much with the time you have on the weekends. Stay calm, you can only go to one or two places in a day, so pick a place or two and go see what's there. Go to places with larger volume for the most part, but don't discount the smaller sales.

When you go shopping, take your time when purchasing an item. If you find something you like, and it's a little more than you wanted to pay, put it on hold. Meanwhile, keep looking around. If you really want it chances are it will be there when you go back. The $35 you save this weekend, added to a few extra here and there throughout the month, could add up to more than a hundred at the end of the month, and then a purchase of a premium piece is in order. When you build up your cash, your collection will grow sensibly. With this attitude will come rewards like that Civil War drum.

Another reward came recently, but only after observing someone else's retribution. In Gettysburg last summer, we were showing part of the collection at one of the July 4th shows and selling off a few items to be able to add to it, when the brother-in-law of a dealer from Philadelphia at an adjacent table brought in a Horstmann sword for that dealer to sell. It

Civil War drum
Identified to the 9th New York Heavy Artillery; $185 in 1997.

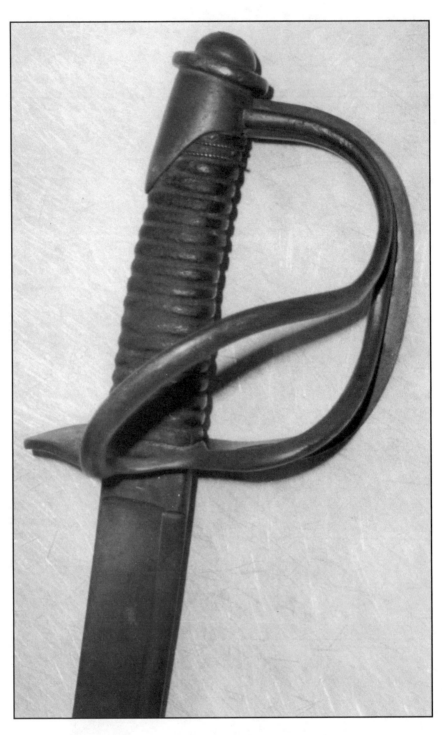

Horstmann sword

was a beautiful piece, fully engraved and well preserved, but Horstmann was misspelled! What does it mean? Draw your own conclusions!

In any case, the sword alone was worth something, and that was the asking price: $550. Not the $800-$1,200 that a perfectly engraved Peterson, for example, would command, but then again the perfect example doesn't have a misspelled maker's mark on it. Another man who really, really wanted to buy that sword, was told about the Horstmann misspelling. But, he had to have it and went to two or three bank machines to get the cash. When he returned with the cash, just as the show was closing, the Philadelphia people sold it to him.

The next day I found him and his very angry wife in a local antique store trying to authenticate the weapon and to locate the people who sold it to him. Talk about retribution! It just wasn't what he thought, and it sure wasn't on a budget. It wasn't the $1,200 piece for $550. What he purchased was just a $550 sword.

My Horstmann sword, for example, came about six months later. It dates from 1840 and is plain, unengraved, but sports the proper marks.[1] I paid $395, and according to popular lists is worth $500-$800. This is one of many examples of rewards given in this book when "collecting Civil War on a budget."

As you can see, this narrative is for collectors who want a return for every dollar they spend; have an interest in the Civil War or early American military; and budget a certain amount of money every week to spend on their hobby. Just apply the strategies described to your own collecting experiences, and it will help make collecting Civil War antiques basic and affordable for you.

Notes

Chapter One

1. James Hatcher, Irving Koslow, Scott Specialized Catalog of United States Stamps (New York: Scott Publishing Company,1994), pp.13–21.
2. Francis A. Lord, *Civil War Collector's Encyclopedia* (Harrisburg, Pa.: Stackpole Books, 1963), pp.134–37; Stanley S. Phillips, *Excavated Artifacts from Battlefields and Campsites of the Civil War* (Ann Arbor, Mich.: Lithocrafters Inc.,1974), pp. 8–9, 98–99, 116–17; Fletcher Pratt, *Civil War in Pictures* (Garden City, N.Y.: Garden City Books, 1955), p. 134.
3. Virginia War Museum, "The Civil War In Newport News, Virginia," America's Civil War, X (July1997), 57; Russell Rulau, *Standard Catalog of United States Tokens, 1700–1900* (Iola,Wis.: Krause Publications Inc., 1997), pp. 466, 500, 606.
4. James D. Horan, *Mathew Brady, Historian with a Camera* (New York: Crown Publishers, 1955), pp. 21–22; Fletcher Pratt, *Civil War in Pictures* (Garden City, N.Y.: Garden City Books, 1955), p. 158; L.A. Godey, *Godey's Lady's Book and Magazine* (Philadelphia: Godey, 1866), p. 458.

Chapter Two

1. Richard Friz, *Official Price Guide to Civil War Collectibles* (New York, N.Y.: Ballantine Books, 1995), pp. 235, 243.
2. Alan Axelod, *The International Encyclopedia of Secret Societies and Fraternal Orders* (New York: Facts on File, 1997), p.156; James M. McPherson, Editor, *The American Heritage New History of The Civil War* (New York: Viking Press, 1996), pp. 471, 478; Robert G. Athearn, *American Heritage Illustrated History of The United States*, vol. 8, The Civil War (New York: Choice Publishing Inc., 1988), pp. 296–97; William Ganson Rose, *Cleveland, The Making of A City* (Cleveland, Ohio: World Publishing Co., 1950), pp. 319–20; Geoffrey C. Ward, Ric Burns, Ken Burns, *The Civil War, An Illustrated History* (New York: Alfred A. Knopf Inc., 1991), p. 188; R.S. Yeoman, *A Guide Book of United States Coins* (Racine, Wis.: Western Publishing Company Inc., 1991), pp. 91–92.
3. Sally Luscomb, *The Collector's Encyclopedia of Buttons* (New York: Crown Publishers, Inc., 1967), p. 43; Stanley S. Phillips, *Excavated Artifacts from Battlefields and Campsites of The Civil War* (Ann Arbor, Mich.: Lithocrafters Inc., 1974), pp. 64–67.

Chapter Four

1. Carl W. Drepperd and Marjorie Matthews Smith, *Handbook of Tomorrow's Antiques* (New York: Thomas Y. Crowell Co., 1953), p. 210.

2. Justin M. Sanders,"alt.war.civil.usa FAQ V2.07" (internet: jsanders, 1994), part 4.
3. Turner E. Kirkland, *Dixie Gun Works Catalog* (Union City, Tenn.: Pioneer Press, 1997), p. 585. Howe wrote the *United States Regulation Drum & Fife Instructor's Book* and reprints are available here.

Chapter Five

1. Ron G. Hickox, *Collectors' Guide to Ames Contract Military Edged Weapons: 1832–1906* (Union City, Tenn.: Pioneer Press, 1992), pp. 18–20, 26–27, 62; Harold L. Peterson, *The American Sword, 1775–1945* (Philadelphia: Ray Riling Arms Books Co., 1991), pp. 80, 81, 121.
2. Peterson, p. 80.
3. Hickox, p. 26.
4. Anthony Carter, and John Walter, *The Bayonet* (New York: Charles Scribner's Sons, 1974), pp. 44–47.
5. Carter and Walter, pp. 44–47.
6. Ibid.
7. Ibid.
8. Ibid.
9. Norm Flayderman, *Flayderman's Guide to Antique American Firearms and Their Values* (Northbrook, Ill.: DBI Books, Inc., 1994), pp. 453–54, 459, 461, 463.
10. George C. Neumann, *Collector's Illustrated Encyclopedia of the American Revolution* (Harrisburg, Pa.: Stackpole Books, 1975), pp. 30–33.
11. Carter and Walter, pp. 44–47.

Chapter Six

1. William B. Edwards, *Civil War Guns* (Harrisburg, Pa.: Stackpole Books), pp. 28, 108, 261.
2. Edwards, pp. 66, 67, 68.
3. David Featherstone, *Weapons and Equipment of the Victorian Soldier* (Poole-Dorset, England: Blandford Press, 1978), pp.13, 36.
4. Ned Schwing, *1998 Standard Catalogue of Firearms, Collectors Price and Reference Guide* (Iola, Wis.: Krause Publications, 1998), pp. 336–38.
5. Schwing, p. 336.
6. Featherstone, p.15.
7. R. L. Wilson, *Colt's Dates of Manufacture, 1878 to 1978* (New York: David Madis, 1985). Purchased this from the Colt Heritage Museum in Gettysburg in 1996.

Chapter Seven

1. William C. Davis, *Brothers in Arms* (New York: Salamander Books, 1995), p. 53.
2. Francis A. Lord, *Civil War Collector's Encyclopedia* (New York: Castle Books, 1965), pp. 225–26.

Chapter Eight

1. Lillian Smith Albert, and Kathryn Kent, *The Complete Button Book* (Garden City, N.Y.: Doubleday, 1949), p. 405.
2. William K. Emerson, *Encyclopedia of United States Army Insignia and Uniforms* (Norman, Okla.: Oklahoma Univ. Press, 1996), pp. 42–43.
3. Lillian Smith Albert, and Kathryn Kent, *The Complete Button Book* (Garden City, N.Y.: Doubleday, 1949), pp. 403–8.
4. William C. Davis, *Brothers In Arms* (New York: Salamander Books, 1995), p. 75.

Chapter Nine

1. Justin M. Sanders, "alt.war.civil.usa FAQ V2.07" (Internet: jsanders, 1994), part 4.
2. Francis A. Lord, *Civil War Collector's Encyclopedia.* (New York: Castle Books, 1965), pp. 85–91.

Chapter Ten

1. Harold L. Peterson, *The American Sword, 1775–1945.* (Philadelphia: Ray Riling Arms Books Co., 1991), pp. 114–19.

Bibliography

The American Civil War, 1861–1865. Alexandria, Va.: Time Life Books, 1994.

Catton, Bruce. *Mr. Lincoln's Army*. Garden City, N.Y.: Doubleday & Co., Inc., 1962.

Civil War Collector's Price Guide. Orange, Va.: North-South Traders, 1996.

Drury, Ian, and Tony Gibbons. *Civil War Military Machine*. New York: Smithmark Books, 1993.

Echoes of Glory. Alexandria, Va: Time Life Books, 1996.

Edwards, William B. *Civil War Guns*. Harrisburg, Pa.: Stackpole Company, 1962.

Emerson, William K. *Encyclopedia of United States Army Insignia*. Norman, Okla. and London: University of Oklahoma Press, 1997.

Falls, Cyril. *Great Military Battles*. London and New York: Spring Books, 1969.

Flayderman, Norm. *Flayderman's Guide to Antique American Firearms and Their Values*. Northbrook, Ill.: DBI Books, Inc., 1994.

Friz, Richard. *Official Price Guide to Civil War Collectibles*. New York: Random House, 1995.

Godey, L.A. *Godey's Lady's Book and Magazine*. Philadelphia: Godey, 1866.

Hickox, Ron G. *Collector's Guide To Ames U.S. Military Edged Weapons: 1832–1906*. Union City, Tenn.: Pioneer Press, 1992.

The Horse Soldier Catalog #24. Cashtown, Pa.: The Horse Soldier, 1996.

Kennedy, Francis H. *The Civil War Battlefield Guide*. Boston: Houghton Mifflin Company, 1990.

Lord, Francis A. *Civil War Collector's Encyclopedia*. Harrisburg, Pa.: Stackpole, 1963.

Luscomb, Sally C. *The Collector's Encyclopedia of Buttons*. New York: Crown Publishers, 1967.

Nicholls, Florence. *Button Handbook*. Ithaca, N.Y.: The Cayuga Press, 1943.

Peterson, Harold L. *The American Sword, 1775–1945*. Philadelphia, Pa.: Ray Riling Arms Books, 1991.

Reedstrom, Ernest L. *Bugles, Banners and War Bonnets*. New York: Crown Publishing, 1986.

Scott Specialized Catalogue of United States Stamps. Sidney, Ohio: Scott Publishing Co., 1990, 1994.

Steffen, Randy. *The Horse Soldier 1776–1943*. Volume 2, 1851–1880. Norman, and London: University of Oklahoma Press, 1992.

Traister, John E. *Antique Guns*. Hackensack, N.J.: Stoeger Publishing, 1996.

Windrow, Martin, and Gerry Embleton. *Military Dress of North America 1665–1970*. New York: Charles Scribner's Sons, 1973.

Wyckoff, Martin. *United States Military Buttons of The Land Services 1787–1902*. Bloomington, Ill.: McLean County Historical Society, 1984.

Yeoman, R.S. *A Guide Book of United States Coins*. Racine, Wis.: Western Publishing Co., Inc., 1991.